SICK & TIRED

BREAKING FREE

YVONNE GONZALEZ

All Scripture quotations are taken from the New King James Version, © 1979, 1980, 1982, 1984 by Thomas Nelson, Inc. Used by permission. Scripture quotations marked (NIV) are taken from the Holy Bible, New International Version ®, niv®, © 1973, 1978, 1984, 2011 by Biblica, Inc. ® Used by permission of Zondervan.

ISBN: 979-8-9858247-3-5

Printed in the United States of America

Kingdom Publishing & Productions, LLC

Book Cover: J. Garcia (RDMR Customs)

Dedication

This book is dedicated to my girls. To The many sacrifices, the tears cried, and many times you just did not understand, it was your love that always pushed me through.

To my mom and two dads that without them there would be no me and to every man or woman who may read this book and be inspired to break free and gain the strength in God to continue moving forward.

To you reading this book be inspired, take it one day at a time, don't be so hard on yourself, with Jesus in front it does get better, WE DO RECOVER!

To my sister Vero whom I admire and love with all my heart. We did it little big sis Generational curses have been broken.

To my little brother Jose and sister Roxanne, I love you both and thank God that he protected you and covered you always.

I Love you

Yvo

Acknowledgements

I want to acknowledge my Lord and Savior, Jesus Christ who through I can do all things because He strengthens me, who without I would not be ALIVE today?

To my Pastor Katherine Aguirre whom I thank God for because if it had not been for her love, prayers, and comprehension I would not be writing this book today.

To Bishop Eric, thank you on so many different levels for your support, your counsel, your prayers, and most importantly your unconditional love. I thank God for you Mr. Miaggi.

To my church family whom without question, embraced me, lifted my hands when I didn't have the energy to lift them, and never ever judged.

I want to acknowledge every surviving family member of every person that has lost a loved one to addiction and or domestic violence- my love, heart, and prayers are with you always.

-Yvo

Endorsement

Pastor Yvonne is an encouragement to the body of Christ. Her raw and transparent story is an open book for you to see how women of this caliber can break THROUGH!!

This story is a benchmark for others to navigate through the adversity that is set before those not just with a powerful calling but for those that conquer with CHRIST!!

It takes an open book like this. It takes the details that we can often overlook and dismiss. It takes the reminder that the many challenges that we have to face in life is what makes us distinct and allows us to walk in dominion POWER!

I thank God for women like Pastor Yvonne that NEVER GAVE UP! Even through the darkest night and uncharted territory. She pushed through it all so that she can share with the world the power that comes from our brokenness and humility!

We all get "Sick and Tired" but truth be told not all have passed through this triumphantly. Which is why this story and encouragement is being so boldly shared with you now!!

I have always been on the side of catalyst's like Pastor Yvonne because I am also a firm believer that RECOVERY IS POSSIBLE!!!

There is always a better way— and this is the way, to point you to Jesus Christ because He empowered us to live a VICTORIOUS life here on earth.

This book is for you.

~Christina Cruz-Mendez

Table of Contents

Foreword

Impactful. Truly a transformative story. A story that highlights God's love, mercy, and compassion. A story that engulfs the reader's soul. A story that will leave the reader in tears. A story that will make one reflect on the self. It is a story of a woman that struggled and found someone that changed it all; Jesus is His name. Having the privilege to read such a hopeful and inspiring book it took me back to the first time I met this woman of God. I am humbled to be able to have witnessed the growth in this woman of God. I have witnessed and am honored to have seen the journey to recovery in the life of Pastor Yvonne. She has and continues to allow God to transform her life. I am so excited to see what God will do through every word, every chapter in the lives of all who read

"Tired of being sick and tired."

Pastor Katherine Aguirre

INTRODUCTION

I was tired of being sick and tired! Struggling with addictions stemming from trauma as far back as my early childhood.

37 years of age a single mother of twin teenage girls and damaged goods. It is the year 2007 and I'm tired of dictating my own life, going in circles, and ending up in the same place (insanity at its best). Yes! tired of being sick and tired with nowhere to turn and no one to run to. Here I am at the end of me. A sudden stop, yes, my personal "rock bottom".

The beginning of a journey I call my journey to recovery. But recover what? Recover all the enemy stole from me! On this day in September, I took my first step and admitted that I was powerless, that my life was unmanageable and that I need intervention. The moment I opened my heart and gave God total access to walk through me and turn on the light on all that was dark in me. One would think this was the end of my struggles, that the moment I surrendered my life it would be peaches and roses, but on the contrary- it was the beginning of a process by which I would have to journey through with God and God alone. It would be the beginning of my journey to recovery.

CHAPTER 1

Digging Deep

I can close my eyes and be taken back to age 5-6 in the south Bronx and remember a home filled with love, laughter, lots of families, and much salsa music. Saturday morning cartoons were papi's favorite. I can smell the bacon, seriously smell the bacon cooking and the fried eggs in the kitchen as mami is waiting for papi to come with the Italian bread from the corner bodega so we can gather around the kitchen table to have breakfast together before papi would head out for his workday and we would have a day with mami cleaning the house and moving furniture around (this was almost religion at our apt in the Bronx).

Our home was normal. Mami did not work out of the house. A young mother 19, a housewife who took care of all our needs and papi up at 4am getting his day started before it was time to ride us to school. Every afternoon papi would pick us up and ride us back home on his motorcycle where mami would be waiting to sit with us to help with our homework. There was nothing unusual about the way we were growing up. This was your typical Puerto Rican home in the south Bronx in the 70's.

Back in those days, it was typical for families to live near one another or in the same apartment building. Our abuela and abuelo (mami's parents) lived upstairs, and my tia's and tio's did as well. It was like living in a huge house with all the family nearby. We were remarkably close to our cousins and holidays were huge family gatherings with the traditional lechon, arroz con gandules, ensaladas and lots and lots of liquor. I can close my eyes and still hear all the ladies in the kitchen, the kids all up and down the hallways, and the men of the family in the living room drinking (it's like music to my ears). It was normal that the men would gather away from the ladies as the woman chatted in the kitchen. There was nothing unusual about this at all, not even that during these gatherings the adults visited the bathroom more than usual. I can vividly remember how there would be a punch bowl every year specifically made for us kids, spiked and we all looked forward to it (it was the only time it was ok to innocently let the kids get tipsy). Nothing unusual about our holidays. By the end of the night papi would have drunk too much and would come home too drunk to remember how he got in his bed. This seemed to be normal at our home except mami would always seem to be disappointed. This was the beginning of what would lead up to a series of events that would be generational.

I can recall as the years past things were changing, papi was now spending more time out the house, he would come home at times withdrawn and, on many occasions, he wreaked of beer. Mom did a great job trying to cover the fact that they had argued. On occasion papi would come home so drunk that he would tear apart the living room. Mami had a living room filled with ceramic statues and I would find her cleaning the mess papi made the night before as he would come home drunk and would smash them against the living room floor in his drunken rage.

I can recall one huge fight where things escalated, I may have been about 7 years old, and I could hear mami and papi arguing in the room as I sat on a bicycle in the dining room and mami was crying as she came out the room threatening to leave to abuelas house. The arguments had become so routine at this point that I was in the center of them as though nothing was happening. I can remember that this day the argument was different. Mami locked herself in the bathroom and papi attempted to get in the bathroom while pushing the door he physically hurt Mami and she began to cry in a pain-stricken voice, I can recall as if it was yesterday the feeling of fear for my mom, begging her we leave to my abuelas house. Papi had come home on another night so drunk that he went in his dresser draw and exposed a gun he kept for safety and pointed the gun at my mami in what he thought was play and as he pointed the gun to her head uttered the words "what if I blew your brains out". The gun was not on safety and before he could blink it went off and by seconds the bullet grazed mami's head. I remember that night mami ran out the apartment in a night gown to my abuelas house (dads' mom) who lived upstairs and refused to return. Papi cried like a baby that night as he sobered up and realized what had just happened and begged mami to return. The arguments and the fights did not stop they would only get worse as the years went by. Adultery would plague the home; the holidays were becoming dreaded for mami as addiction to drugs would now lurk and ravage our home. Papi's behavior was become harder to manage, papi would come home at 6PM after a day working all day and he would close the shades in the apartment and not allow us to leave the apartment as he was turning down for the night and would tell mami that if anyone knocked at the door looking for him to tell them he was unavailable. Papi was spending more time away, he now was out in social clubs with a band of musicians.

The 1970's marijuana, tye dye, mushrooms, acid, cocaine, and heroin were prevalent that they had begun to take hold. At the end of 1969, there were more than 100,000 heroin addicts living in NYC. Drugs had become glamourous, celebrities were doing them, and people believed they were cool. It was the thing amongst major music celebrities in the 70's. famous musicos like Hector Lavoe, Willie Colon, and many latin artists. It was the disco and salsa era and papi had become part of that culture.

Our home was in disarray mami would spend the nights out gambling at her friend's house simply to distract herself and not come home to her nightmare she would spend the night out claiming she had a headache and was unable to drive. She did anything to stay away from home as she did not know what to expect from papi anymore.

This only made matters worse and for more arguing. I can recall one afternoon I had become ill and Mami would ask papi to drive her to the hospital and while we were in the back seat papi was driving wreckless under the L train on Westchester ave because he was drunk, he and mami began fighting in the car, mami telling him we wanted to arrive alive to the hospital and papi would become enraged.

On another occasion I can recall sitting in my abuelo's 3rd floor apartment as they sat on the fire escape, I hear abuelo tell mami that papi had just driven up and his brand-new shiny mustang was totaled due to his drunk driving. Papi was drinking more.

It's the late 1970's and Mami now hears from a tia was involved with cocaine, drugs were something new to mami, she didn't understand the effects and later would learn what heroin had taken over. One morning as mami was cleaning on a typical Saturday she looks up in the drop ceiling and finds a rubber arm band along with a syringe. Mami no longer decides to be tolerant and threatens to leave for good but because of the honor and respect she had towards her mother Abuela Mercedes and her marriage vows mami stays a little longer.

Reflection: there is power in vulnerability, secrets don't keep you sick, they kill you.

1. why do I keep doing the things I do?
2. why have I been attracted to the type of people with whom I have been in a relationship in my life?

3. why do I react in certain ways in certain situations? Where did my behavior patterns come from?

4. where did my behavior patterns come from?

5. why do I sometimes feel lonely; helpless; desperate; scared; angry; suicidal; etc.

This is the first step in the healing process, starting to ask these questions. It's a healthy start wondering about the cause-and-effect dynamics.

CHAPTER 2

Turning Point

It's now the year 1977 and mami's mother/Abuela the pillar of her life becomes ill. Abuela experiences a heart attack that she would not recover from. Mami's foundation was rocked, and her whole life was about to change. Abuela was the glue in my mom's life and a loss that would devastate her for years to come. Mami would never grieve, mourn or heal from the loss of her mother.

In the summer of 1977 Con Edison system is hit by lightning, a massive power failure plunged New York City and most of Westchester County into darkness in sweltering midsummer weather. Stradling millions and disrupting communications. Firefighters were slowed down, looting was evoked, trains stopped, Bronx house of detention was on fire. I was 7 years old and can remember like it was yesterday that as the lights went out papi got up from bed, got dressed to check what was happening, he came back into the apartment to report to my mom what was taking place and that night papi grabbed his gun and he sat outside our apartment at the top of the steps the entire night to ensure that we were safe and that no one would make their way into our apartment.

It's funny as I am now 50 years old and the memory of what papi did that night is vivid within me. I can still feel what I felt that night knowing that papi was sitting at those steps and we were out of harm's way, because my hero, the strongest man I knew was protecting us.

As I sit writing this, I am consumed by the wave of emotions taking place, how the same man that caused uncertainty and at times fear would be the same man that would be a safety blanket for a little girl.

A couple of months later Mami after threatening to leave would gain the courage needed to pack and make a move. She did not tell anyone where we were. Mami, I am not sure if she had a plan or had hope for a door to open towards freedom moved us to a friend's house. This was not a place where you would take your children and feel comfortable, but I am sure that Mami at the time in her desperation to escape the roller coaster she was living felt that this was her only way out from the abuse and the hell of the effects of addiction she was living. Papi is determined to find us, my abuelo mami's dad discovers where we were and convinces my mother to come back home.

Mami decides to come back home with my dad's promise that he would change for better, but the promise was vain. My abuelo relocated to Puerto Rico and soon after my mother makes the decision to move with him, but not until after she meets a man that would sweep her off her feet.

Reflection: as children reacting to life out of emotional trauma we adapted to defenses to try and protect ourselves and to get our survival needs met, this led to further traumas that led to wounds. Let us become aware of cause and effect. Let us become aware that we have emotional wounds from childhood that we need to get in touch with in order to stop them and heal so that they can stop dictating how we live life as adults. This must be done by revisiting our childhood.

In your reflections journal continue being a detective, take a good look at yourself and ask yourself.

1. Where did that reaction come from?
2. Why am I feeling this way?
3. What does this remind me of from my past?
4. How old do I feel right now?
5. How old did I act when that happened?

Get to know yourself, get honest, and see yourself clearly. So, let's be Inspector Gadget in our inner process so that we can change the programming.

CHAPTER 3

Summer Affair

It was summertime, I can recall the kids playing in the neighborhood, the pompa open, the sound of jump rope, mister softee music playing, kids playing in the parks, and riding their bicycles.

Mami takes my sister and me to the park to ride our bicycle and once we arrive, we are greeted by a man on a bicycle whom mami introduces as her friend. It becomes apparent as we spent the day at the park that mami's new friend and she were extremely close. I must have been 7 or 8 my sister was about 5 years old, and the memory of this day is so vivid in our minds today. As I wrote this book, she and I read the chapters together and we compared the memories and it was clear the negative impact, and the trauma that was left from having experienced these events would scar our lives for years to come. As I continue to take you through the journey of my life, of our lives you will see how the choices that were made by the adults in our lives had a negative impact on our childhood and who we would become as adults.

My sister and I never discussed what happened at the park and I know for certain it took me days to not think of it. Several days later we were all outside, a typical summer day in the Bronx. As the day is ending the parents are all gathered as usual in front of the building as everyone in the Bronx in those days was like family. Not like today where you can live in a building for years and never know the person next door. In the 70s in the Bronx, everyone knew one another, adults knew everyone's child, and neighbors were more like tios and tias.

On this afternoon as the parents gathered, I can recall being in the circle where they all were. Mami and papi, all their friends but on this day it was different. Mami's friend we had met in the park was part of this circle. As I looked around, I remember the anxiety, panic, and fear that rushed through me. I can recall like I am standing in that circle today the thought (if papi finds out that mami was with this man, he will kill her). What weight for a 7-year-old to carry! These concerns caused anxiety disorders as the years went by. The concerns began to affect my sleep, created fears and social anxiety that as time went by only worsened.

My mami was having an affair! The man she was with had given her a sense of confidence she had not felt in a long time. She began to see life differently and wanted to get away from the nightmare she was living with papi. The fights at home escalated, papi was drinking more, and he was hiding out more than before. There were more knocks on the door in the evening when papi would come home to settle for the evening. As usual, Mami was to tell everyone he wasn't home. Papi would come home drunk and decide he wanted to cook and one night as we all slept, he turned the stove on to cook and fell asleep and Mami woke up to smoke in the apartment and we were all covered in ashes. It was by the Grace of God we didn't die that night. I can recall Mami threatening papi that she would leave, and he never took her seriously. Until one day she came home with plane tickets to Puerto Rico for all of us. Papi still was in denial that she would leave until the day came that he had to drive us to the airport.

It is 4 AM and papi is driving us to the airport, my sister and I in the back seat. As papi is driving us to John F Kennedy airport he cried like a little boy, he begged mami not to leave him, and he promised that he would do better. As I watched papi cry, I hoped that mami would change her mind and that papi would turn the car around and we would all go back home

I was not sure what exactly was happening, but I knew enough to know that the rest of our lives would never be the same again.

Reflection:

What is self-reflection? It is the process of getting to know yourself internally. It is getting comfortable with understanding the workings of your thought, wants, desires and mind overall. It is normal to get comfortable with your external reflection. You know what you look like and who you are physically. Light hair or dark? Blue eyes or brown? Long hair or short? These are all things we know about ourselves. But self-reflection is the process of getting to know yourself internally.

Often, this is a more difficult thing to do… which is why guiding self-reflection questions can be so helpful.

To help you engage in this process of self-reflection, I have curated a list of questions to ask yourself. There are no right or wrong answers to these questions, so don't be discouraged if you have difficulty answering them at first. Sometimes self-reflection questions can be uncomfortable. As you explore new areas of your mind, uncomfortable thoughts and feelings may come up.

These self-reflection questions are meant for you to dive into looking at your past, which can be uncomfortable but It's important to push past any discomfort that may arise to get the full benefits of asking yourself the reflection questions!

"You are beautiful. You are worthy. You are enough.".

1. What is your first memory?

2. What was your relationship like with your parents growing up?

3. Do you have any blatant childhood trauma that comes to mind?

4. What is something you have overcome?

5. When was the happiest time in your life? Write about it in detail.

6. Would you change anything about your past if you could? Why or why not?

7. What is the most valuable life lesson you've been taught? How did you learn it?

8. Who did you spend the most time with as a child? What was that relationship like then? How is it now?

Write a letter to your past self... What would you say?

CHAPTER 4

On The Run

L a Isla del Encanto Puerto Rico 1977-78, Aeropuerto Luis Munoz Marin. Mami's friend picks us up and this will be the beginning of traumatic events that would affect our lives for years to come.

As I researched for the preparation of this book and the edification of all that would come across it. The information provided you are about to read I learned reading an excerpt from another amazing book "broken children, grown-up pain" and my prayer is that it will assist in explaining how our childhood wounds and environment affect our childhood brain leading us to live lives in lack of wholeness.

After further research, I was educated that The Thalamus is your body's information relay station, the place where all your body's senses except smell are processed before being sent to the brain's cerebral cortex for interpretation. Your Thalamus plays a role in your sleep, wakefulness, consciousness, you're learning, and memory. The thalamus is an egg-like structure in the middle of your brain, like a train station all information must pass through the thalamus first before being routed to its destination in your brain. Your thalamus contributes to perception and plays a role in sleep and wakefulness. In a nutshell this works a lot like the hard drive of a computer. When a hard drive is filled with information (software) the hard drive is now useful. The software of our brains (information) can tell the difference between right and wrong and whether we are wounded or whole.

With, a child who has not matured lacks the chemicals in the brain causing memories to be distorted in turn making the wounds that take place in childhood trigger the thalamus to make its own decision to keep the child from being hurt again. This is based on the adrenaline, the impact of the trauma, or even on the child's experiences. A decision made by the thalamus is not reality. These decisions are not truths.

A child who has experienced trauma will be locked in years to come with not a clear picture of the events that took place Creating strongholds, creating our thoughts to be held captive, living in imagination, locking the child and making the child unable to make decisions all due to Deception of the thalamus.

I say this all to say that because of the decision of the thalamus the rest of my life from this point forward would have been a result of the imaginations and the stronghold created by events and traumas of my childhood that would send me on a whirlwind of lies, heartbreak, unfulfillment, feelings of rejection and lack of love.

As my sister and I sat together comparing our views for this book, we concluded that we did not have the same perception of every event and that our views at times were distorted from the truth which is the result of the thalamus being triggered and creating its own story.

In the bible 2 Corinthians 10:5 tells us that we must destroy arguments and every lofty opinion raised against the knowledge of God and take every thought captive to obey Christ. In 2 Corinthians Paul tells us we have the power with the weapons given to us by Gods power to destroy strongholds and or fortress. There are human thoughts that have been created and locked that we need to take captive. Thoughts that have kept us in bondage.

We are now in Carolina Puerto Rico, and we are at mami's friend's house who by now we know he's her new boyfriend and in order to protect his identity, we will call him Manolo. We then would spend the next few months living at my abuelo's house in the country in Puerto Rico. This would become our new home; we would go to school there and start a whole new life with mami and abuelo until one-day mami tells us she must leave to find us a place to live. My papi had threatened to come to Puerto Rico and remove us from my mother's custody and she would now leave to find a place for us to go to hide us from papi. Mami was gone for what seemed weeks, I cannot recall how long she was gone for. Prolonged separation of young children and parents can be traumatic, potentially resulting in post-traumatic stress disorder and long-lasting impairments in functioning leading to anxiety. Anxiety.org

I can recall vividly the overwhelming feeling of loss and intrusive thoughts, sadness, fear, and abandonment. I remember getting sick to my stomach, nausea, and fear of nightfall every single day mami was gone. I was the oldest of my sister and I tried to not share my feelings for her sake my abuelo was not very compassionate after all he didn't have a clue on how to deal with two little girls. My sister and I made the best of our time in the country at abuelo's house, we attempted to have a childhood as normal as we could after all we were two city girls who were spoiled with the finer things in life to now walking in dirt, picking fruits and vegetables from abuelo's farm for dinner and snacks and having cows and horses as pets. Nighttime was the scariest time living in the country as bats would come out and you could hear the coquis all night not to mention whatever banged against the pelcianas- that's the roll-up windows in Puerto Rico. Anxiety was on high only I did not know what anxiety was- I was only 7 years old and man oh man how much I wish and prayed life would be back to normal, and we would be back at home in the Bronx with mami and papi but, deep down inside I knew it would never be that way again.

On the last night we would be alone with abuelo he had a neighbor over and it was nighttime, my worst time of the day. As we were lying in bed I had a massive headache, my stomach began to hurt, and as I go into the kitchen to tell abuelo what I was feeling I got sicker and began to vomit. Abuelo gave me an aspirin and sent me to bed, and I managed to fall asleep that night only to wake to the sound of screaming, dogs barking and lots of commotion outside. The neighbor that was in the kitchen that evening had experienced a heart attack overnight that killed him. This would be the beginning of my fear and anxiety of death for years to come.

The next day mami would arrive suddenly and she would move us back to Carolina to a safe place where papi would not be able to find us and take us from her. We would go to live with Manolo. Manolo lived in a small wooden house on top of a cement house that was owned by his mother and sister. It became clear as time passed that the sister was not happy that we were there. The sister did not want us to use the bathroom in the house we would now be forced to use the letrina. The letrina is an outhouse, the outhouse was old and dark at night and there was no shower. In the evenings for us to shower we would have to use a hose that was in the backyard and go into the bushes behind the outhouse and wash down with soap and the hose. The house we were staying in was a room where there was only one bed for mami and Manolo, my sister and I slept in hammocks that hung over the bed they shared. At night when it rained, you could hear the swarm of water bugs that would bang against the closed pelcianas and on occasion find their way into the house causing terror until daylight. We lived in fear; mami was concerned that papi would find us and take us away. When mami would leave to run errands my sister and I were forbidden to go downstairs to the cafeteria that Manolo's mother ran and served lunch to the factory workers of the local business. One day while mami was away, we got the dreaded call that my dad's sister who lived nearby had spotted us and was downstairs seeking us, she was with my Abuela (papi's mother) panic went through me, but we had no choice but to go down, after all we were not old enough to make the decision not to.

Eventually, mami would arrive and our tia only wanted to ease my mom's burden and be a part of our life. For a little while, we had a bit of normalcy until we would have to move again. Mami now would move us to another town in Puerto Rico to another family member's home. We would go to a new school (3rd one in less than 2 years). Here we would be surrounded by older cousins who would treat us like little sisters and love on us., but before we could get comfortable, we would have to move to abuelo's where mami would leave us for what seemed months and come back to New York City to establish a home for us to come back to.

Reflection:

1. When did you feel most down/lost? Why? How did you overcome it? If current, how do you plan to overcome it?

2. Do you still maintain many relationships from childhood/your past? Are they healthy? What value do they bring?

3. What's your favorite memory? Why?

4. What's your least favorite memory? Why?

5. Are you happy? Why? Why not?

6. What challenges are you currently facing?

7. Who are the three closest people to you right now? Describe those relationships.

8. When do you feel most alive? Do you make time for that time/thing/place often?

CHAPTER 5

Open Doors

For we are not fighting against flesh-and-blood
enemies, but against evil rulers and authorities of
the unseen world, against mighty powers in this
dark world, and against evil spirits in the heavenly
places.
Ephesians 6:12

John F. Kennedy airport, 1981 I am 9 years old. Mami is supposed to meet us at the airport only she does not make it in time. My sister and I are ushered into a room with security and Mami is being paged through the AP system. She comes storming through the doors and is driving us back to the Bronx to what would be our new apartment.

We are back living in the same apartment building we lived in with papi and Mami, he would still be the superintendent; only now he lived there with his new pregnant 19-year-old girlfriend (papi was 35).

Papi's drug use was ravaging his life and causing major effects to ours. Mami would put herself through school while supporting us on welfare. I recall how hard it was for her and at times we had nothing to eat. Mami would get creative to make sure we never went to bed hungry, she would frequent food pantries, and at times dinner was flour she fried with a little sugar. Papi would refuse to give Mami any support simply to make her suffer for leaving him, only the ones affected were my sister and me. Papi would follow Mami wherever she went and would threaten her every opportunity he could. He would mock her for living humbly and reminded her every opportunity he got of how much she lost by leaving him! He boasted and would let my sister and I know religiously that our lives were much better when we lived with him and that because of her choices we were now living in poverty.

Papi was very prideful, and this pride would lead to destruction in his life. I write this and reflect on how much pride was the root that caused so much chaos.

Scripture tells us that God opposes the proud but gives grace to the humble. Pride is a sin, it is a heart attitude expressed in unhealthy, exaggerated attention to self and an elevated view of one's own abilities, accomplishments, position, or possessions. Pride has been called "the cancer of the soul." Pride, in its sinful form, is the direct opposite of humility, a trait that is highly praised and rewarded by God.

CHARLES SPURGEON -Described pride as an "all-pervading sin" He said, "Pride is so natural to fallen man that it springs up in his heart like weeds in a well-watered garden... It's every touch is evil.
You may hunt down this fox, and think you have destroyed it, and lo! Your very exultation is pride. None have more pride than those who dream that they have none. Pride is a in with a thousand lives; it seems impossible to kill it."

Because of the pride in his heart, Papi would eventually lose everything, his denial of his drug use and the chaos surrounding him would have him now struggling in his new relationship. His new mother to his now 2 children, my brother, and sister would be on the verge to leave him as well and he would go on to be incarcerated and lose his new job, ultimately leaving him homeless for many years to come.

Papi's taunting and desire to see her fail pushed Mami to reach new heights. She would push through college to get a degree and become a professional. With Mami working This would mean we would spend much alone time and on occasion be looked after by older cousins and now be subjected to environments of perversion, incest, lust, and more drugs early in our lives. At the beginning of open doors, we would not be able to close on our own which would affect the next stage of our lives.

Make no mistake about it: pride is the great sin. It is
the devils most effective and destructive tool.
C.S Lewis

A man's pride will bring him low, but a humble spirit
will obtain honor.
Proverbs 29:23

Pride affects us Christians also, we can all pretend to be perfect in church on Sundays in the pews, but we need to take a deep-down look at the very real issues. Did you know that Rebellion, pride, and stinking thinking have ensnared us in affliction?

Reflection:

1. Define pride in your own words
2. Ask yourself are you aware of the pride in your life and how it manifested?
3. Will you identify and write down a few of those areas? And how can you guard against being prideful in those areas?
4. Do you have a personal lesson the lord has shown you about pride?

CHAPTER 6

Skeletons in The Closet

The year is now 1986 I'm a teenager in high school, Mami had dated a couple of men in her life, but nothing serious at all. Our lives seemed normal; Mami had managed to provide for us and give us stability. She didn't raise us with a hard fist but didn't let us run around crazy either. She allowed us to come to her and always spoke to us about life and relationships, she was a friend. Mami tried extremely hard to raise us the best she knew. I do not think she really understood how we were affected by what had taken place up to this point. To be honest, I thought life the way we lived was normal until I began to self-examine and see patterns that made me question my adult behaviors and actions, it wasn't until this point that I would ask why is it that I continue in this cycle. Doing the same things over and over expecting different results. Why is it that even without trying I end up in the same scenarios? Why is it that it seems I'm living my childhood all over again without seeking it out?

Generational curses are habits and behaviors that are passed on from one generation to the next. Mami strived to give us a life better than the one she had but statistics prove that children learn what they live and what they have gathered from generations past. I do not blame Mami for my choices in life because I know she worked hard at ensuring we had a better upbringing than hers, and she never willed me to make the choices I did, but generational curses are passed down through action, our own experience and stories. I realize as an adult I was connected to my past, roots were created and embedded deeper than my childhood experiences. The effects of sin are naturally passed down from one generation to the next. When a father has a sinful lifestyle, his children are likely to practice the same sinful lifestyle.

Mami was a cool mom, she was our friend, there was nothing we could not discuss with her, she gave us counsel; she led us but would allow us to make our own mistakes.

At age 14 I would meet a boy 6 years older than I was, I would lose my innocence at age 14 Mami would not know this, by the time I was 19 I would have been with 2 other boys over the age of 21 and engaged to be married by age 16 this would be a relationship I would be in until age 20. By 21 I would have become pregnant and had an abortion that no one would know about. Mami suspected it and confronted me about it but gave me the benefit of the doubt and we never discussed it again.

Manolo would come back from Puerto Rico and live with us for a short while, except Manolo had another woman in his hometown. Mami and

Manolo would eventually go their separate ways and a short while after would meet my stepdad. This was a hard pill to swallow at first, we were all young women now, and having another man step in was a bit difficult. Eventually, he would make his way into the family, Mami would spend lots of time away from home with him, and we were young women left home alone. Mami had taken on guardianship of two other young women, my best friend who had left her home, and my sister from another mother. Mami trusted us she had open communication with us. We all dropped out of high school, the boys some of us dated were on the street scene, drug dealers, fast cars, and quick money were a part of our world, it was normal it was what we knew. Manolo had introduced Mami to quick money-making when he was around, it was our normal.

Mami was happy. It was great to see her in love after so many years alone struggling, so we accepted Angel- except Angel was married and mom would be the lover. Little did she know how her choices would affect our lives later.

Eventually, I sabotaged my engagement by age 19, I then fell into an even more dysfunctional relationship with a man older than I who also was involved with a woman and had a child. This relationship would prove to be abusive emotionally and physically. It would be one that would not be easy to walk away from. At age 21 I would meet a man who would be my daughter's father. We moved in together; the beginning of our relationship was difficult; we were young but not in love. We worked hard at being a family, but life got in the way. Partying, drinking, drugging, and betrayal crept into our relationship. By the time the girls were 4 years of age we had grown so apart that the relationship was over. I got pregnant again, it was such bad timing, we made the decision to terminate the pregnancy. Neither of us was equipped to bring another child into the world. This was a secret, a skeleton I kept for years. I lived in shame; guilt was something I carried for a long time. Though I did not know truly the biblical implications and truths behind my actions then; I knew enough to know that what I had done was wrong and condemnation had set in. I was living out the consequence of my actions.

My daughter's father and I attempted to make things work but the reality was we were both young with our own childhood baggage, and no true role models and the longer we stayed together the more toxic the relationship was becoming. We attempted to build a home, and we did our best to be a family for the sake of the girls, but it was inevitable. We were living in sin, we were unmarried, living life on life's terms, and we did not stand a chance.

As I gather my thoughts and information, I give God glory and honor because of the fervent and effectual prayers of the righteous avail much.

We had a praying mother whose prayers kept us, kept me.

It is the year 1995 after the termination of my pregnancy I would become ill, doctors would have no idea after much testing what was happening. I was experiencing complications from the termination. I would be admitted into the hospital for evaluation, I would eventually be rushed into emergency surgery as all hell had broken loose inside of me. I nearly lost my life that night and would wake up to the news that I would no longer be able to bear children. Today I am alive because before he formed me in my mother's womb, he knew me, and he set me apart and kept me all the days of my life.

My secret, the one that caused me so much shame the one I vowed to never share nearly took my life that evening.

My daughter's father and I would not recover from the damage to our relationship and eventually went our separate ways. This decision was not an easy one but necessary.

As I continue to take inventory of the journey writing this book, I want to stress the importance of prayerfully asking the holy spirit to walk through you and show you the areas in your lives, that perhaps you still have not surrendered to him and the significance of repentance and renouncing.

For the first time as I am fearlessly searching, I am looking at myself honestly, I have had some hesitation in putting these things down on paper, but shame no longer has a hold on me. I have avoided looking at myself honestly, sweeping things under the rug for years to forget. I am letting my skeletons out of the closet, it's time to release the secrets that have kept me sick and bound.

I wasn't a Christian when I terminated my pregnancy, but I know there are many women like me in church hidden grappling with haunting cycles of shame and regret despite what we know about sin, forgiveness, and grace.

I pray that today if you are a woman who has had an abortion you understand that repentance is necessary. Yes, abortion is a sin, it is a grievous offense against a holy God and our only hope is to repent and believe the gospel. God offers us his grace, he offered me his grace, but we must heal, I needed to heal and know how to heal. To you reading this, abortion is trauma, it devastates the body and the soul. It takes a knife to our image-bearing nature as life-givers. I did not really understand the shame that so often haunted me, I put a band-aid over the wound and pressed on the bleeding to stop the pain but never dealt with the infection that was festering beneath.

I know God forgave me, but I did not forgive myself. There were issues that manifested as a fruit in many ways: anger, depression, anxiety, and endless striving to name a few. Although I didn't understand biblically, I knew that what I had done not once but twice was killing a human being. The Bible is not silent on this matter it has a great deal to say about the value God puts on life and even when life begins.

King David illustrates this most beautifully in his famous psalm.

For you created my inmost being you knit me together
in my mother's womb. I praise you because i am
fearfully and wonderfully made; your works are
wonderful; i know that full well. My frame was not
hidden from you when i was made in the secret place
when i was woven together in the depths of the earth.
Your eyes saw my unformed body; all the days
ordained for me were written in your book before one
of them came to be.

Psalm 139

Life is Life, it is precious, no matter if it is one day or 100 years on this earth. Even in the womb God sees life, he values it, he is the author, and he has ordained all the days of its life just like he did with me, just like he's done with all of us. I did not understand then what I do know now. God knew me before he formed me, I should have not been alive today satan tried to take me out before I could be born, he knew what God had deposited in me, he knew the purpose God had created me for, he did not only try to kill me at birth, but he attempted to take the life of my mother, the woman that God chose to carry me. What an amazing God we serve. If we simply understood that we have been created by God and solely for the purpose of God, we would value life.

We are the sheep of his pasture says psalm 100:3:

Know that the Lord is God. It is he who made us, and we
are his, we are his people, the sheep of his pasture.
Psalm 100:3

This is what the LORD says-Your redeemer, who formed you in the womb: I am the LORD, the Maker of all things, who stretches out the heavens, who spread out the earth by myself
Isaiah 44:24.

The Bible has dozens of scriptures referencing the value of life, and how humanity is given, not earned. God is God alone and only God has the authority to decide life.

I learned that Jesus isn't shocked, he knew my secret, he knew my story, he knows every hair on my head, and he took the crushing shame and insurmountable pain off my shoulders my father washed me, in grace and set me free.

To you reading this book today my prayers are with you, and I pray that, if you have had an abortion or know someone that has, please know that I may not know your circumstance or story, but Jesus does. There is no place you can hide from him; I want you to know that the same way he was not shocked by me he is not shocked by you either. Come to Jesus and repent of your sin, after all; there is no secret place that he cannot see you declares the Lord in Jeremiah 23:24, he goes on to say, "Do not I fill heaven and earth?"

You can run, but you can't hide. It is pointless to try and hide from a God that knows all, a God who is everywhere, a God who knew you before you took the action that you were going to do it.

Who can hide in secret places so that I cannot see
them?" declares the Lord. "Do not I fill heaven and
earth?" declares the Lord.
Jeremiah 23:24

In Genesis 3:9 But the Lord God called to the man, "where are you?

Why would a God that knows everything, that is everywhere call out the man as though he did not know where he was? God is everywhere (omni-present)!

God knew that Adam had disobeyed but gave him the opportunity to tell him for himself, he gave him the opportunity to come clean. God already knew the answer.

Then the Lord God called to Adam and said to him,
"Where are you?"
Genesis 3:9

Adam goes on to answer, "I heard you in the garden, and I was afraid because I was naked, so I hid." Here we hear how Adam is in hiding afraid because of his sin and ashamed.

God knows where we are always, he knew what we were going to do before we did it, But God is such a gracious God that he gives us the opportunity to come clean, to come to him in repentance, he gives us free will. God is a gentleman he doesn't push himself on us unlike how our society likes to make it seem.

To you reading this today, our father God is giving you and me the opportunity to come to him unashamed but repented. To you who reads this; the same way God washed me clean, the same way he removed my grave clothes is the same way he wants to do it for you. God wants to wash you clean in grace and set you free once and for all of the guilt and the condemnation that does not allow you to move forward.

Please know that you are fully known and loved by God and understand the beautiful part that when we repent and receive his grace your child is waiting for you with Jesus. You will see them again tomorrow like I will see mine again tomorrow "one day in his courts is 1,000 years on this earth".

Is anyone among you sick? Let them call the elders of the church to pray over them and anoint them with oil in the name of the Lord.
JAMES 5:14

I encourage you today that if you have had an abortion turn to the elders of your church, the leaders, and or ministers that you can trust and open.

You do not have to do this alone. Find and join a bereavement group, join an abortion recovery group, and find a hurt and hang-up recovery group. You do not have to live with pain, guilt, and shame like I did. God can and wants to use your story to set another woman free and save the life of a child. But first, he wants to free you from the shackles that have kept you bound.

Be liberated today, receive forgiveness from God, and confess your sin with a humble heart and contrite spirit. I want to bring you help, healing, and hope from your brokenness God can and wants to forgive you, you don't have to live in condemnation any longer.

"if we confess our sin, he is faithful and just
to forgive us our sin and to cleanse us from
all unrighteousness."
1 John 1:9

Forgiveness is available to you; salvation has not been revoked.

1 John 1:9 says, "if we confess our sin, he is faithful and just to forgive us our sin and to cleanse us from all unrighteousness." Even the sin of abortion.

For you that say or think you can't forgive yourself like I didn't, I want you to know this is a lack of faith in God. By saying this we are telling God "Your sacrifice is not enough for this sin". When we do this, we negate the power of the sacrifice of Christ in our lives.

Reflection:

1. What secret did you say to yourself you would take to the grave?
2. What secret are you keeping that has made you sick?
3. What secret keeps you living in shame?

4. What is keeping you from forgiving yourself?

5. Are you looking at yourself honestly

CHAPTER 7

Insanity

It's the year 1999 I relocated to Florida with the girls. I was at the start of my career, family, and independence. I was single and was dating nothing serious. About a year after being here in Florida I met a man we will call Junior to protect his identity. Junior swept me off my feet, and we fell in love this was different it was life as an adult. We moved in together after about a year and I couldn't be happier. The first year of us living together was my dream come true I wanted to spend the rest of my life with him. Junior was divorcing but was fully invested in us. As time went by, I learned Junior had more children in NY I didn't know they were not a part of his life; his son spent weekends with us, I was determined to bring our families together so that he could heal from his past, there were some things about Junior's past that were unclear. Junior shared with me the story of how he grew up and the tragedy of his parent's break up and how his mother abandoned him. Junior's separation and the beginning of his divorce were ugly the stress and the pressure would lead him to start drinking. At first, Junior was having cocktails, I didn't see anything concerning but before long he started slacking in his business affairs, Junior was self-employed, and he handled his own business affairs. The drinking was out of control it began to take a toll on our relationship. Junior got arrested for DWI more times than I could count. Our finances were tied up in lawyers and bail bondsmen, he was unable to stay out of jail. I was exhausted, and Junior was becoming verbally abusive and feeling insecure about my work relationships. He was becoming dangerous in the sense that he couldn't rationalize and would take risks. I tried everything I could to help him keep his business afloat and make sure he stayed out of jail, but it was inevitable abuse crept into our relationship. December that year Junior had come home drunk, the girls were with family, and I didn't want to stay and deal with what was coming with his drinking. I decided I would spend the holiday with my family. As I am driving us home- I tell Junior who is in the passenger seat that I was going to drive to my family for the holidays he starts to argue, and the argument escalated, Junior lifts his hand while I am on the highway, the car in motion, before I could think, he backhands me. I manage to make it home devastated and as I am attempting to park Junior snaps and with his closed fist begins to strike me several times. I recall taking my hands and covering my head for protection when suddenly some bystander witnessed the scene. It happened that the witness was an off-duty sheriff, that evening Junior was arrested. Junior would spend the holidays incarcerated; I was subpoenaed to testify against him. An order of protection had been placed between us. Eventually Junior would come out of jail, and I would drop the charges.

I moved out and went to live on my own, but I still wanted to fix him. I cared about him, and I rationalized his behavior, I tried to fix him. I afforded him the opportunity to come to stay with me after assisting him to get into detox. I didn't want him on the streets. Junior got out of detox and never recovered, he would never quit drinking and now moving him out was not on the horizon. One holiday weekend I gave him an ultimatum and went away with the understanding that he would be gone when I got back. While on the getaway I receive a call from the county jail that Junior had been arrested. I would only take one more call from Junior who stated he was not going to plea bargain his jail time and would enter an addiction program offered by the county for substance abuse recovery that would help with shortening his jail time.

I would receive letters from him I never read, I would not accept his calls and on two occasions I visited him to ensure he was ok and would not be in contact again. Junior and I would go our separate ways.

I continued the insanity cycle doing the same thing over and over expecting a different outcome. I wanted nothing more than to fix him. I wanted nothing more than to see him be the man I knew sober. What I didn't understand was that he needed to want it more than I did. I attended Al-anon, a recovery group for the family of those that are affected by addiction, but it was one-sided. Junior attended AA only because he felt pressured that our relationship would be over and because it was court mandated. I don't believe he ever really tried to stay sober. Alcohol had taken over the man I once met but little did, I know that this was not his first time around. I later learned that he had been in long-term recovery from addiction, and alcoholism which led to the loss of his family. I admit now I was in a physically abusive and very toxic relationship. I got to the place I was tired of being sick and tired, I hated lying in bed with junior, alcohol wreaked out his pores, and I no longer wanted to be his partner, but I hesitated to leave for fear of abandoning him during the toughest time of his life fearing that leaving him would be detrimental and that I would be abandoning my dad all over again. A result of my very own traumatic event.

The trauma experienced when my mother left my dad at the age of 7 was repeating itself- it was a cycle. I carried guilt and pains that were not mine to carry. None of what I experienced belonged to me. I was broken from childhood experiences. I wanted to make up for what happened to my father. I wanted to save papi all over again.

As I journey in this recovery process, this healing journey, releasing all my fears honestly, as I do this inventory of what is embedded deep within, the holy spirit has revealed how domestic violence and chaotic events are linked to my traumatic childhood. Watching a parent be physically injured, watching a parent be abused has severe implications. Domestic violence is about power and control from the abuser. Abuse distorts love, Junior turned love into a weapon instead of a sacrifice.

Traumatic events don't always leave physical scars, but they often leave emotional and psychological ones.

Those imprints can affect a child's mental and physical health for years to come and adulthood. Not everyone gets the support they need in childhood. As adults, we may still be dealing with the emotional and physical consequences. Limited understanding and experience and inadequate skills for processing make the immature mind traumatized.

Some examples of traumatic experiences are:

- Divorce of parents
- The sudden death of your grandparent who lived with you.
- Getting bullied in school for stuttering.
- ETC.

We tend to label these as non-events, but what if we could go back in time and remember how we really felt and thought during those events?

Trauma is a distressing, painful, and or shocking experience that causes harmful psychological, physiological, and spiritual effects.

At times we think well that was not a major event, it was something little, but the reality is it may not have been so little. As adults when we look back at painful events from our past losses, hurts, rejections, violations, or abuse- we look at them through adult lenses, normalizing them while intellectually minimizing the traumatic experience. This strategy tricks us into thinking the event had little impact, then ignoring it and acting like it was not such a big deal.

I thank God for the opportunity to write my story and do an inventory of events I had swept under a rug and be able to journey in my healing and through this journey be able to reach someone who perhaps has not unlocked a memory that may be linked to childhood trauma.

My prayer today is that if you are a woman or a man who is experiencing domestic violence, you run because it doesn't get better. I also want you to know that domestic abuse can occur in non-physical ways. As a victim of abuse, you can be abused in other forms such as verbal, economic, emotional, and sexual to name a few.

If you find yourself in a domestic abusive relationship do everything to get out. Don't keep it to yourself, don't be ashamed to get out, and please do It safely. Please note that domestic violence has severe spiritual implications. Every story is a different one. If you are being abused counseling is not an answer, don't fool yourself into thinking getting counseling while together is an answer not until the abuse stops and you have undergone individual counseling will this be a solution. If you are in an abusive relationship, please do not be ashamed, IT IS NOT YOUR FAULT! Your abuser may have told you that you provoked it, this is a lie and it's manipulative. Violence is never an answer. God's desire for our lives is healing and wholeness for our lives. If you are being abused, please reach out to your Pastors, Elders, or Ministers. Do not suffer in silence. I know starting over is scary but staying in an abusive relationship is scarier and he or she is not going to change without intervention from God. YOU CAN'T FIX HIM OR HER only God can.

Domestic abuse is a leading cause of injury and death to women worldwide. Nearly one in four women around the globe is physically or sexually abused in her lifetime. Relationship abuse is ugly, even and especially when it comes from the people we love. Please note that domestic violence abuse is a learned behavior, Men who batter learn to abuse through observation, experience, and reinforcement. Your batterer may be a good provider and a respected man in his community or church. There is no one type. Alcohol and drugs are often associated with domestic violence, but they do not cause it. An abusive man who drinks or uses drugs has two distinct problems; substance abuse and violence which must be treated.

Please do not make excuses for him or her. There is often nothing a domestic abuse victim can do to change their abuser. YOU CAN'T FIX THEM their change must be independent of you. Get the help you need, there is hope for healing from the aftershocks. Please know that God loves you deeply and wants you to know you are not defined by your trauma, your circumstance, or your brokenness. It is difficult to admit abuse but so necessary.

You lived and you survived, God rescued you, his hand was upon you, his hedge covered you, you are not reading this by accident and now it's time to heal. YOU CAN'T FIX THEM!

There are 6 things the Lord hates -no 7 things he detests: haughty eyes, a lying tongue, hands that kill the innocent, a heart that plots evil, feet that race to do wrong, a false witness who pours out lies, a person who sows discord in a family."

Proverbs 6:16-19 NLT

Reflection: In your reflections journal take the time out to self-reflect and ask yourself some starter questions.

1. How did I get into this mess? Was it love?
2. Why did you stay in the relationship? Was it fear?
3. What has kept you from starting the process of healing from your abuser? Is it shame and embarrassment?
4. What traumatic event did you label as not a big deal?

Self-reflection will help us identify areas that we can address as we seek healing. I pray that when you self-reflect, God will grant you the knowledge to change the areas in your life that need his healing and that you allow him the access he needs to come in and do the heart surgery he is longing to do in you.

CHAPTER 8

Denial

Falling apart is not an option for me. I must keep going at all costs. No time for failures I have people looking at me, I have these babies I need to care for. I have a career I must maintain, there is no time for distractions. My girls are depending on me. Things were going well; peace set in; No time to worry about Junior anymore. My baby sister came to live with me now, and I get to forget my hurts and pain by helping her and her baby get on their feet and engulf in my work.

It's the year 2002 I meet a man by the name of Eli. He invites me to dinner, quite the charmer, an older guy. We began seeing more and more of one another and before long our friendship bloomed into what I thought was a relationship. Eli managed to become a part of my world in a short period of time.

As I sit here allowing the Holy Spirit to pull out from the root anything and everything that serves me no good purpose, I am being honest and owning my story, I shake my head at how I just ignored every red flag there was with Eli. Eli would give me all the world offered materialistically but never gave me what I wanted most (his heart) betrayal was a constant, he didn't know how to love, I was simply just a conquest. Eli was charismatic, quite the charmer but the amount of emotional abuse I endured in this relationship was more than I could bare. Eli never stopped making sure we were cared for, caring for the girls and myself was a strategy and a priority but settling down with me was not something he was ready to do. Eventually, the emotional abuse that I endured in this relationship led me to begin to numb my pain. I turned to substances to find solace. I don't blame Eli, nor anyone else it seemed I kept running around in circles, numbing the void I felt within, with sex, drugs, and alcohol to name a few trying to fill what I call a God hole. A God hole is impossible to fill if not with God himself.

What exactly is a God hole? a "God-shaped hole" in the human heart, a terrifying bottomless abyss opening inside us which we would do anything to fill, a famous modern metaphor for the yearning in the human soul that drives us on a spiritual quest. The "God-shaped hole" is the innate longing of the human heart for something outside itself, something transcendent, something "other." Ecclesiastes 3:11 refers to God's placing of "eternity in man's heart." God made humanity for His eternal purpose, and only God can fulfill our desire for eternity. This desire, this longing can only be fulfilled by God, and therefore likened to a "God-shaped hole." The problem we see, though, is that humanity ignores this hole or attempts to fill it with things other than God.

Jeremiah 17:9 describes the condition of our hearts: "The heart is deceitful above all things and beyond cure. Who can understand it?" Solomon reiterates the same concept: "The hearts of men, moreover, are full of evil and there is madness in their hearts while they live..." (Ecclesiastes 9:3), we can't trust the desires of our hearts. The New Testament concurs: "The sinful mind is hostile to God. It does not submit to God's law, nor can it do so" (Romans 8:7). Romans 1:18-22 describes humanity ignoring what can be known about God, including presumably the "God-shaped hole," and instead worshiping anything and everything other than God.

Sadly, that God-shaped hole is what keeps us chasing, and seeking, and too many of us spend our lives looking for something other than God to fill our longing for meaning through business, family, and relationships but in pursuing these things that are not eternal, we remain unfulfilled and wonder why our lives never seem satisfactory.

Please understand that void of paternity and the lack of encounter with God can keep us in a place of never arriving due to feelings of Rejection, hidden insecurity, fear, Self-hatred, feelings of inadequacy, and loss of confidence at one point or another in our lives that have made us feel small and insignificant.

As I continue my inventory and take off this mask, I wear so tightly I recall how I began to hang out with friends, a life of late-night parties, lots and lots of alcohol, and drugs just crept in! It's insane as I think of how all this began and how it's not something I even liked at first but seemed to keep me numb to the reality that the man I had trusted, thought I loved, and allowed into my world was not as devoted to me as I to him (rejection). I sought love although I told myself a different story. On the outside, I put on a facade of someone who had it all together but deep down inside I was in shambles. The truth was I was scared, lonely, tired, and full of rejection, feeling as though I was not good enough or visible and needed to be rescued. I can recall one night I sat on my living room floor, surrounded by people, I could hear voices, I heard and participated, but I was alone in a room filled with people. I recall that I'm still there sitting on my living room floor wanting to call out to my Mami for help. I looked at her and with everything inside of me, I wanted to cry and say, "Mami I'm tired of living, I can't do this by myself, and I'm tired of pretending, please help me, please take all my issues and help me get well"! but pride got in the way. I was living in a world full of comparison and goals and achievement and was living from there. I didn't have an identity, I couldn't let anyone know that I didn't have my life together, that I had failed, and I had driven myself into a wall, I was crashing fast, but failure was not an option. I had to keep putting on this façade, I couldn't take off the mask of self-confidence, the mask I wore so tightly, the mask I designed to hide what was deep within, the mask I wore to hide the person I wanted no one to see. There was no way I could let Mami see the strong independent, successful woman she raised me to fail.

Partying and getting high was my new normal, my money got tied up on drugs, and often I was too high to sleep and must get high to stay awake and function. My life had gotten out of control, I was spiraling, and spent all my money on drugs. Eli was giving me more and more money but the more he gave, the more I spent on drugs. He was clueless, after all he only came on occasion to spend the night.

Depression kicked in and I didn't even, know it. One morning my doctor sits with me and wants to discuss depression, it was something I couldn't admit. My doctor was relentless in getting me to hear her. She testifies about her very own battle with depression and manages to get me to open. She stops at nothing to get me to go to the hospital, she sends a fax to my job that states "IT IS A MATTER OF LIFE AND DEATH FOR YVONNE TO GET TO THE HOSPITAL". Today as I think of this day and the way my boss who received the fax looked at me and told me to go in a hurry, I realize this was divine intervention. God's love was pursuing me, he was recklessly after me, think about this! what doctor goes out of their way to break all HIPPA laws? My doctor gives me specific instructions for the emergency room and before I knew it, I was admitted. I was against going to the hospital to be admitted but deep down inside I just knew it was necessary I knew enough to know that I was in a depressed state; so, against my own logic, I agreed. My stay at the hospital was an interesting one Eli came to visit me that night and didn't take my condition seriously, in his words I was lovesick and just needed to go home, but it was then that I had an awakening to the fact that it was time I let go of what was truly destroying me and that was "ME" and my own desires. To Eli, I was just another trophy that validated his existence. I managed to get discharged after evaluation, I was prescribed medication I vowed never to take and challenged myself to better mental health and make changes. There was no way I could take my life. My girls were watching, I had no choice but to make it- suicide was not an option for my girls needed their mother.

I realize the Lord's hand and covering have been with me always. Even when I had no relationship with him, he protected me, I didn't know God, but he knew me and had a plan for my life. Even when I attempted to take my life, when I was reckless with his temple, the father loved me so much that he never left me. I could have been dead, I should have been dead, but God's mercy and his grace kept me. My father God held me by my hand even in my blindness, he removed the scales from my eyes. Today I see how for years I searched for the love of my earthly father in all the wrong places without recognizing the love of my heavenly father was with me all along.

I pray that you who are reading this understand that insecurity and rejection leave us feeling empty and we struggle to achieve and succeed. There are barriers in our lives that make us feel less than and you don't have to feel this way because our heavenly father is everything we need, and he's never left us.

My prayer is that you understand paternity and identity, that you understand that the betrayals and the divisions come from the lack of receiving the father's love. Because of past rejections, there are wounds that have become infected in our lives, wounds that are still open and we need the lord to heal our open wounds so that we may tell the story of our battle scars with our heads lifted high.

My prayer is that you understand that rejection, unforgiveness, and the fragments of abuse that stem from these places make it difficult for us to receive the love of the father that is without condition. To you reading this, the father loves you and you don't have to be a certain way; you don't have to perform or pretend because God the father is sufficient. My prayer is that you accept your father's love, the love that he so freely gives us in your life, and that you understand there is nothing you must do for him to love you. We go through unnecessary trials because we have the void of fatherhood and God's love. May you walk in God's love from today forward and let it hit you every day. To you reading this please understand that you are the apple of God's eye, and you no longer have to continue with the mask on. It is ok and time to cut the ties that hold the mask so tightly, come to Jesus just as you are, and watch how the very things you covered up shamefully you will proudly use for the father's Glory and honor.

Reflection: Take a moment and pause on your God-shaped hole and be vulnerable today.

1. What have you tried to fit into the God-shaped hole that didn't fit
2. What was the outcome of fitting something other than God in your hole either permanently or temporarily?
3. What are you hiding behind your tightly fastened mask?
4. Are you ready to take off your mask? Why and or why not?

CHAPTER 9

Rock Bottom

Tired of being sick and tired is an understatement! Here I am After years of struggling with addictions stemming from trauma as far back as my early childhood running from myself.

I'm 37 years of age. A single mother of twin teenage girls and damaged goods. It is the year 2007 and I'm tired of dictating my own life, going in circles, and ending up in the same place (insanity at its best). Yes! tired of being sick and tired with nowhere to turn and nowhere to run. At the end of me, a sudden stop, hitting the wall. Yes! my personal version of "rock bottom" is a very painful place. This crash was painful in every way, and I finally had no choice but to face myself brutally, painfully, and honestly. My darkest hours.

It's the year 2007 and I am invited to a woman's church service where I would surrender my life and will over to Jesus Christ. The beginning of this journey to recovery. But recover what? What was I recovering? I would quickly learn that I was on a journey to recover my identity! The one that was given to me by my father, the very identity satan was after since before I was born. On this day in September, I took my first step towards it and admitted that I was powerless from everything that controlled me and dictated my every step, powerless to what was influencing me that was not Godly. I was powerless and my life was unmanageable, and I needed intervention. On this day I surrendered, I laid down the weight I carried, and I turned it all over to Jesus. I opened my heart on this day and gave God total access to walk through me and turn on the light on all that was dark within me. I was ready for change; I was intentional about the change I needed in my life. There was no halfway in or halfway out. I knew I needed something different; I didn't like my condition or where I was, so I knew I had to be deliberate. Thinking back to when I was in Florida after the breakdown, endured I pictured my daughter's grandmother always speaking of God and reading the bible to me years earlier and the joy that resonated through her. I can recall like it was yesterday the sadness deep down in my soul, and I needed what she had. I would say to myself "I want to feel what she feels" My thoughts were, here is this woman, alone, doesn't have a husband, her son has moved on, but she is always full of this amazing Grace. "I NEED THAT". I needed change! I was desperate and for some unknown reason just kept thinking of her and wanted what she had, although I did not know what that was at the time. My life was dysfunctional, I was living in bondage, wrapped up in grave clothes and needed liberation.

As I think of, the woman with the issue of blood, the account in Mark 5:24-34 and Luke 8:42-48 the woman with the issue of blood is a tough passage for many people to understand. This woman suffered for 12 years before she was healed by Christ. Doctors were unable to heal her and due to her constant bleeding, she was deemed unclean by the Jewish people because of the Law (Leviticus 15:25-27). This woman as a result of her condition was an outcast.

As I think of my condition and the stigma, many people judged me, and I placed labels on myself. I didn't see there to be a change for me. I looked for healing in men, I looked for healing in people pleasing, I looked for healing in codependency, careers, and anything I thought could take the pain away.

I needed the newness of God, I needed the peace of God, I pushed through the obstacles I was facing at the time and ran to the only place that was left for me to run to. It's sad but true for so many of us that the place we need to run to is the last place we go to. That day I ran to the altar, I can recall my Pastor's words. "Is there anyone that wants to turn their life over to Christ?" He said it again, actually a few more times as I can remember that with every repeat, I was in a struggle within myself "should I go? Should I not?", he said it one last time and this time I knew I just couldn't miss the moment. I ran to the altar that morning, I can't remember what was said to me that day, but I do remember the tears that flowed, I can remember the weight being lifted off me. I will never forget the relief I felt that day and the knowing that I wanted more of it. God met me right where I was at rock bottom. It was on this day that I said "God I can't anymore, I give it to you, take control of the wheel because I can't do this anymore.

It was like the woman with the flow of blood, she knew she had come to the end of her, she just knew that Jesus was passing through and that she had tried it all and that she could not miss the moment, she believed that if she just touched the hem of his garment that she would be healed. I stood there that day as the Pastor made the call and just knew that I could not miss the moment, that I had to push through the crowd and touch him.

Like this woman I had exhausted all my resources, I had tried it all, I had spent years in a vicious cycle, living with hurts, hang-ups, and habits doing it my way at rock bottom.

I recognize today the power in my surrendering all to God, surrendering the power in my calling the shots in my life, surrendering control of the family, my finances, my life, and how it released God's power. On this day I offered myself and my body as a sacrifice and said yes to God changing my conformity in this world and renewing my mind.

Years later I look back with immense gratitude for the incredible gifts that my crash bestowed upon me. You might think I'm crazy for saying this, but I'd do it all again, in a heartbeat, for the incredible insights and growth I gained through what was my darkest hours. I learned some solid lessons and wisdom worthy of sharing.

Therefore, I urge you, brothers and sister, in view of
Gods mercy, to offer your bodies as a living sacrifice,
holy and pleasing to God-this is your true and proper
worship.2 Do not conform to the pattern of this world
but be transformed by the renewing of your mind.
Then you will be able to test and approve what Gods
will is- his good pleasing and perfect will.
Romans 12:1-2

My prayer is that you reading this understand that there is power in surrender, something happens when we are intentional when we come to Jesus humbly. God wants nothing more than to take the wheel in our life. Our father and creator did not create us to suffer. My prayer is that you understand the power in surrendering unconditionally, laying down everything, and giving it all to Jesus. I pray that you understand the power of giving up responsibility to God. God doesn't want us partially; he wants us totally. Today I pray that as you read this that you are honest with yourself and you ask the lord to forgive you if you have held on to dreams not his for you, visions and plans that didn't include him and that today you recognize that you have hit a wall and once and for all just open your hands and turn everything over to him. My prayer is for you that has not surrendered and are reading this that you cry out to the father and surrender your life and will not just with your words but also your actions. Today I pray you unconditionally walk into the newness of God totally surrendered, withholding nothing so that you can experience the joy and peace that God the father has for you and begin to walk in the purpose of you and your life.

Reflection: As you pray unto the father today, examine yourself with the help of the holy spirit and ask the Lord to show you the areas in your own life you have bargained with or hold on to. Take a moment to realize that you are off course and that your life choices have gotten you to this point and declare today once and for all to never again accept such mediocrity from yourself. As you reflect list some of the things that you are holding on to that you know God has asked you to let go of and or list the things you know you must surrender to the Lord in order to take the forward step you need for your life.

Ask the Lord to finally reveal the dysfunctional behaviors so that you can come out of the denial radar and no longer cleverly delude yourself into thinking everything is fine and end up being built on a big fat lie and false foundation.

Reflection: At this point gain fresh perspective, become self-aware disempower your patterns and behaviors, and break the mold by reflecting on everything you thought to be true.

Using your reflections journal be true to yourself and write down Your motives, others' motives, your beliefs, your fears, the why you did the things you did and the ones you didn't do, the why you attracted certain people and circumstances and the why you succeeded and why you failed. Right here take a moment to reflect and self-examine in raw detail and from this point begin to build again from the ground up with a fresh perspective and a renewed sense of clarity.

1- What was your rock bottom?

2- What has the Lord revealed to you to let go of?

3- What are your motives for not letting go?

4- What big fat lie have you been telling yourself?

5- List some of your dysfunctional behaviors.

CHAPTER 10

Run but You Can't Hide

It's 2008 I have overcome so much, I surrendered my life to Christ, I got Baptized in water, and I've decided to give myself totally to the Lord. It's a new journey I'm excited about. I've changed, people, places, and things. I transitioned back to New York, and I am doing things differently for a short time but not before long I would make the decision to marry who I thought was the final detail of this newfound way of life. My person, my happily ever after! Convinced marriage was the answer and not wanting to fail God, I convince myself this was the way. We had a shotgun wedding, all the red flags were present, and all the reasons to not get married were there but I turned the cheek. I wanted what I wanted when I wanted it. It became clearer and clearer as we drew closer to the wedding day that this was a mistake. I knew before the wedding that I didn't want to go through with it but because of shame, I pushed and went through with it. I remember our wedding day, we were supposed to exchange vows, but he was still too hungover from the weekend to have words to put on paper, it wasn't till we were at the sanctuary that he tells the pastor he didn't have any words written. I could have turned back at that point but my own strongholds, my own selfish desires, and meeting my own needs kept me moving forward. I knew enough to know I was making the biggest mistake of my life.

The man I was about to marry whom I had only known for a few months had tons of baggage of his own that now combined with my baggage became very heavy to carry. Now here we were two train wrecks colliding, married, running from the truth (ourselves), and not facing the man in the mirror. My new husband secretly trying to stay sober from 25 years of an addiction that was killing him and me in denial of my very own demons, in desperate need of owning up to the fact that I needed saving. As I journey through this book, the reality is that this has been my very own Journey to recovery. Here I was in self-defeating behavior doing the same thing all over again. Sick as the secrets I harbored, the secrets killing me, attempting to live a functional life (denial at its best). The honeymoon was over the first week of marriage if there ever was one thinking about it honestly was over. Betrayal and infidelity lurked in their dreary head and the reality of what we got into was slapping me in the face. HOW DID I GET INTO THIS MESS?

LOVE! Most people I know marry for love. I certainly did! Or did I? My concept of love wasn't as clear as I thought it was. This concept was influenced by others' perceptions of who I was or the perception I wanted others to have. Keeping it real it was performance-based. The truth was, I didn't love who I was or even saw myself as important, due to past experiences in my childhood and teenage years. In addition to those experiences, my parents weren't around to nurture my sense of self-worth. This all led to a faulty concept of love which made it extremely difficult to tell the difference between healthy love versus sick love. Self-inflicted shame and embarrassment are being affected by what other people will think to back out now, the spirit of pride at an all-time high.

It's now 2011 and we were now on this journey together. Christians in recovery from childhood traumas of divorce, broken homes, parents on drugs, infidelity, adultery, abuse, and domestic violence, sexual immorality to name a few. We are both regretting many decisions, questioning our love for one another, and battling our own demons Yet through all this, we find favor in God's eyes. I have learned that God never wastes a hurt, God will take what the enemy meant for evil and turn it around for Good. It was in our brokenness, in our worst pain and struggle, it is here The Lord places a vision in my heart, a burden for a recovery ministry. God took the pain and anguish I felt for my dad's passing, combined with what I was now enduring with my husband, and turned it into my greatest passion. He laid a burden upon me. I took my pain and joined God in his cry for his people.

I can recall as if it were yesterday, sitting in my home church, looking around the different pews and seeing all the beautiful people, the couples all dressed in their Sunday best, hair perfect, smiles as though they were in a fairy tale book, happily ever after. I close my eyes today and recall the anguish I felt in my chest as I sat there alone. Alone because after being married just a few months my new husband had left home; addiction came knocking (relapse). My husband would run off. Drugs, binges, women, parties, and weeks away from home became normal.

I kept a secret one that was killing me! I Came to church smiling but hiding the reality that the house I desperately tried to make a home of was filled with darkness. Week after week I would go home to the reality of a husband who was addicted to drugs and indulging in women and stayed out for days at a time, even months until the streets beat him up and he'd come home under the condition that we never spoke of it. I would agree to not talk about it for his sake, harbor my hurt and pain, I would clean him up, pray him back to life and attempt to move forward never addressing the issues and believing it would get better. I had this huge secret that no one knew, one that was breaking me down more and more, with every relapse, I would be left and relapse after relapse losing my worth more and more. When he was gone id numb my own pain in entertaining conversations of the opposite sex. When he would come home, we walked around my house with this pink elephant in the middle of the living room, pretending it wasn't there.

Fear of judgment, fear of finger-pointing, shame, and embarrassment kept me silent. This couldn't be happening to me! How could I be going through this? I was educated, and independent I knew better, I didn't need this in my life were some of my questions, but I held on. We see this often, satan the accuser who comes to steal, kill, and destroy would have you live in shame to keep you from everything God has for you.

How could this be happening to me? because I wasn't ready to accept the fact that I was a victim. Accepting that fact would mean having to face my shame. I did not know then that I was living in the deception of the evil one. satan kept me captive for many years bound with the "what would people think of me syndrome."

Interestingly as I sit here writing and reflecting! I can vividly remember the loud voice in my head saying, "These people will never understand your life," the loud voice that I know now is not from God, shamed me! This same voice kept me from backing out of this marriage.

I should never have gone through with It! Here we are wedding weekend, my family was in town, my husband exchanged text messages with another woman, he got high all weekend and I knew then that I should have canceled everything Yet too concerned about what people would say as they were celebrating a wedding that was to happen, I turned the other cheek and continued with the wedding thinking I could fix him, this will all change later. Only to receive a text message a week later from yet another woman whom my new husband of 1 week was in an affair with, another woman with children. It seemed this was a pattern.

I battled in silence with myself. The reality of my allowing this kept me in bondage portraying the happily ever after marriage, performing! My own selfish motives.

One night after a long run and nowhere to turn. I cried to God on my knees Exhausted from wearing the mask and putting on a façade, Tired of Smiling and holding on believing God for a miracle he heard my cry. This voice I know now to be the voice of God said "Yvonne, there are people just like you, hiding behind the clothes and smiles afraid to speak up because of the stigma attached to their own struggles.

I looked around the church that day and can still see what I saw that day. The perfect picture smiles but is broken inside afraid to talk about their very issues.

I remember like it was yesterday that as my husband was gone and deep down inside, I wanted him to stay gone the holy spirit did not allow me to leave him lost to die on those streets. I remember today that I would head out to the streets to go rescue him from the hell he had placed himself in. I was fed up; how could I have gotten into this mess? I wanted to be free from having to deal with the hell I was living in, I did not want to take him home, physical, verbal, and emotional abuse was too high of a price to pay. On one occasion my birthday, my husband had come back from having been on a binge, he comes with a birthday cake and begins to argue, and we get into a physical altercation that night and he left.

Eventually as usual he comes back. I can recall as if it were yesterday that I requested a meeting with our new Pastor and confessed our story. I will never forget the miracle that happened when I picked up my husband from a long run, he was disheveled from having been out for weeks. His face was disfigured to the point he was told he would need minor reconstructive surgery. As we sat in the hospital room a man, a Christian man walked over to us and spoke with my husband. This man shared information on a local Christian recovery ministry. During our meeting fed up as I was, I looked at our pastor and handed him the card and asked the pastor to investigate the place for us and how I thought this was ideal for my husband. Pastor although new to what we were facing loved us from the start and believed in God for intervention in our lives.

I tell my pastor that my husband needs to go away to an inpatient recovery program, that he/ my husband needs to go and recover (I wanted him gone). My pastor disagrees! I am frustrated and disappointed. Disappointed because of The anger deep inside no one saw, the lack of respect and self-seeking ways were destroying me. My husband was struggling badly, he didn't know how to love himself, let alone another person.

Our pastor at this meeting looks at us both and says, "what you need is Jesus". Confused and feeling defeated at the same time all I could think was "we already have Jesus; we are already in the church and that isn't working". I was Clueless that we were on a journey with Jesus, that he had begun a process of transformation, that divine intervention had begun in not just my husband's life, but mine. God was at work in our lives. I realize today that while I was desperate to fix my broken husband God was more concerned with fixing me.

For the next few months, my husband would get sober, we would be regulars at church, I gave myself totally to the Lord, and I was seeing the wonder-working hand of God. I must say that What I had in mind about recovery is not at all what recovery is. I would learn via this season of my life that recovery is a journey, not a destination, and that it's also not the same for everyone, everyone's rock bottom is different, this was not his, but this was mine.

My husband would be sober for a year, He would relapse several times, and he would leave and move on to another relationship, but God kept strengthening me. I was getting stronger and stronger in God, and the vision God placed deep down in me would begin to ache to be birthed out, it would take form. As we embark on this journey of our own, we begin walking in ministry. Delivered in New Faith Recovery ministry is birthed from my greatest pain and anguish, this ministry was one that would change my life, my husband's life, and the lives of many. God begins to use us in facilitating groups for his glory even in through our own struggles for his glory. My husband through this ministry and our own submission is now sober and healing, we begin marital counsel for all the dysfunction of our marriage even through an order of protection. God was on the move in our life. I won't say we didn't struggle in our years in ministry because we did, but the Lord held us down and as long as we stayed connected to him, no weapon formed prospered. The Lord began to heal me, I no longer tried to be everything to my husband, I Let go and Let God and for 11 years we facilitated groups and saw God's hand in everything we did. We surrendered our will for him, we allowed the Lord to lead our lives. I will speak for myself when I say that the Lord began to heal me from the hurts and hang-ups of the betrayal endured in my marriage, from the abuse, and eventually with much counseling, I was able to forgive and press into what the Lord was calling me to do. In 2017 after the death of my mother and attempting to heal from that my stepfather becomes ill and I must stand front and center of that, we are ordained Pastors. In those years, we faced many challenges, my husband struggled with the ministry, he would leave several times, but find his way back! I held on to God believing that what he did once before in our marriage he could do again, but the difference this time was that my husband had given up and I was too exhausted to keep fighting. I don't make excuses for my actions, but the 2019 pandemic came, I was going through the motions, and I became drained, frustrated, and didn't have the will to continue. I cried to the Lord to have his way. I shifted my prayer and asked God to intervene I knew I didn't want to fail the father and walk away from my marriage, so I turned it over to him.

The pandemic came and we were quarantined, a door into our home was left open, and I was too fatigued to fight. Depression entered; we were under spiritual attack but too weak to fight. My husband had given up and was headed in a different direction. Spiritual warfare was unleashed, and we did not have our armor on.

The Bible says that satan roams around looking for whom to devour, he comes looking to steal and kill and he had his way. There was a crack unsealed and the enemy took advantage. Domestic Violence entered our home during a very vulnerable time and attempted to take both our lives in the blink of an eye. But t I am here today to say that what the enemy meant for evil God turned it around for Good. I am telling my story today; it didn't have to be this way. It could have been different, I could have been dead that day, and my ex-husband could have been incarcerated but God intervened. His love, his mercy, and his Grace were all over both of us. I praise God today because he covered me, protected me and he answered my prayers. What satan meant to destroy us both, God is using for his Glory.

It's almost 2 years since I've been divorced, God had his way in my life and my situation. My husband walked out one day while I was at church and decided to move on. I exercised my right and filed for divorce. I thank God for being in the midst of our situation, I am forever grateful that he protected my heart and that his peace was with me, I owe God everything for his saving Grace and healing hand.

I do believe in marriage; nothing will ever change that. But marriage takes two people. God designed marriage and marriage comes with a label (much assembly required). It takes a lifetime of work to put together marriage the right way but most of us plunge in without reading the instruction manual.

God designed marriage it Is his idea, he defined it in Genesis 2:24 in the garden of Eden he reiterated it in Mark 10:6-8 But from the beginning of creation, Go, made them male and female therefore a man shall leave his father and mother and hold fast to his wife, and the two shall become one flesh, so they are no longer two but one flesh. God created the first man, Adam, he said, "it is not good for man to be alone. I will make a suitable helper for him" Genesis 2:18. God created male and female bodies and souls to complement each other in such a way that they become "one flesh" in marriage.

God's design for marriage is that it be a unique union between a man and a woman in a covenant for life. He designed that the consummation of sex only be between a married couple any sexual expression outside the marriage is a sin. God's design for marriage is an unbreakable covenant such as God has made with his people. God pronounced marriage very good Genesis 1:31.

God's covenantal design for marriage is broken by abuse, and scripture does not mandate that an abused wife or husband must remain married to an abuser; therefore, the body of Christ is called to model God's compassion toward abused men and women through effective strategies designed to meet the needs of women and men who are trying to escape abusive relationships. God designed marriage so that spouses could experience companionship, physical relationships, respect, love, and caring. On the contrary, abuse and neglect are condemned by scripture and can break the marriage covenant. When this happens, divorce is permitted due to the hard-heartedness of the abuser and as legal protection for the abused.

As I write this, I must say that in the face of abuse, divorce is a complex decision that requires physical, spiritual, and emotional support. Our churches need to be educated and model Christ's compassion toward abused women through effective strategies designed to meet the needs of women who are trying to escape abusive relationships.

I thank God for the support I received from my pastoral family as they executed effective church discipline during this time of crisis. And provided care, safety, and counseling. My prayer today is that if you have a similar story, you seek help. That you turn to your leaders.

The US dept of justice (2000) reported that intimate partner violence is pervasive in US society. Approximately 25% of women surveyed were physically assaulted and or raped by an intimate partner at some point in their lifetime. In a 10-country study of domestic violence against women, the world health organization found that 15% to 71% of women disclosed sexual or physical violence by a partner or husband.

To you reading this, if you are a Christian man or woman in an abusive relationship, you don't have to stay there Get out and speak up. God's covenantal design is broken by abuse, and scripture does not mandate that an abused wife must remain married to an abuser.

My prayer as you read this book and journal in your reflections journal is that you do a spiritual inventory, a raw inventory of yourself. That with the help of the holy spirit you allow him to reveal areas that are still dark within you. Perhaps areas your subconscious locked away to protect you. Ask the holy spirit to show you, what about your past keeps you in the mess, the insanity, the insecurity, in the feelings of inadequacy. It's very easy to fall into a pattern of blaming others for where we are and staying there with the woe is me mindset, but when we truly get tired of being sick and tired and we come before the presence of our father intentional, with the desire to be made well memories will begin to be unlocked and with the help of the holy spirit healing will begin in your life if you are truly honest.

Hebrews 5:13 For someone who lives on milk is unskilled in the word of righteousness since he is a child. In other words, we are still babies if we don't understand that through God's word there is the power to cultivate what good seed God has deposited in each of us. God has deposited well in each one of us, he has given us the power to unlock what has us stuck, to not be stagnant, and the power for more. God has left us all that we need to walk in healing and maturity. It's time we stop blaming the world for our condition and allow God to keep digging, cutting, prodding and pruning. God wants us to inspect what is inside and allow it to be revealed. It's time we confront our root systems meaning it's time we check our motives, our values. God wants us to grow he is a God of growth.

Today I thank God because he has allowed me the opportunity to walk this journey and provided a spiritual awakening to see the areas in my life that needed healing. I don't hold hostage any of the persons mentioned in this book. I realize they all played a huge role in my growth. On this journey, I have received Gods peace and forgiveness and in turn rendered the same to all the persons in my past. God has allowed me to do a spiritual inventory and has had me reach the core of my root system and been pruning away at all that does not bare good fruit. God has deposited good in you and today I pray you become aware of the good deposit in you and that you release any bitterness, unforgiveness, resentment, rejection, and every mindset that holds you captive in old mindsets and see that what is inside you is Grand. The potential in you is so huge. Today I pray for transformation in your life and that you don't waste one more second of what God has deposited in you. My prayer is that you are tired of being sick and tired and that you care and cradle what God has given you and receive the new.

Reflection:

Self-reflection Is required for healing emotionally and spiritually from any harmful relationship.

My prayer is that you discover how your abusive actions have affected you and that you understand what happened and work your way to healing.

After reading this take a moment and ask yourself these starter questions you can answer in your reflections journal.

1-Am I holding on to resentment?
2-Am I in fear? Am I using my anger for a positive change?
3-Has what have I gone through crippled my sense of trust?
4-Am I resentful?
5-Have I forgiven? This is the key to healing
6-Have I come to God for healing?
7-What areas do I still need healing in?

I pray that as you have read through the pages of sick and tired you have been blessed and that you have begun your journey to healing and recovery. My prayer is that your reflecting does not stop at the end of this book, but that you continue praying and ask the Lord to continue showing you the areas that perhaps have been swept so deep under a rug that you forgot they were there. I pray that if you don't know Jesus that you invite him into your heart today and allow the holy spirit to transform your life. If you don't know Jesus and would like to make him Lord and savior of your life recite this prayer right now.

God, I recognize that I have not lived my life for You up until now. I have been living for myself and that is wrong. I need You in my life; I want You in my life. I acknowledge the completed work of Your Son Jesus Christ in giving His life for me on the cross at Calvary, and I long to receive the forgiveness you have made freely available to me through this sacrifice. Come into my life now, Lord. Take up residence in my heart and be my king, my Lord, and my Savior. From this day forward, I will no longer be controlled by sin, or the desire to please myself, but I will follow You all the days of my life. Those days are in Your hands. I ask this in Jesus' precious and holy name. Amen.

Congratulations and welcome to the family of Christ! Now find a local bible based church and begin your walk with Jesus Christ, you won't regret it!

I love you but Jesus loves you more!

Pastor Yvo

Connect with Yvonne:

Email: Simpliyvo.com

Instagram: Tree_of_life_lw

Facebook: Yvonne Gonzalez

Made in the USA
Columbia, SC
26 November 2022